SURVIVOR

from dark ... ught

ILLUSTRATED ANTHOLOGY

SURVIVORS' POETRY

from dark to light

SURVIVORS' PRESS 1992

For all survivors wherever they may be.

Special Acknowledgement
Special thanks to Hilary Porter for her
patience and dedication in the collection,
collation and original typesetting.
And thanks to Frank Bangay for encouraging survivors
to submit poems and illustrations.

Publication Data
First Published in 1992 by Survivors' Press
33 Queensdown Road, London E5 8NN

Distributed by Central Books
99 Wallis Road, London E9 5LN, 081-986-4854

A catalogue record for this book is
available from the British Library
ISBN 1 874595 00 3 (paperback)

Editorial Acknowledgement

Front cover illustration by Martin Brownlee

Cover design by Joe Bidder & David Keay

Edited by Frank Bangay, Joe Bidder & Hilary Porter
for SURVIVORS' POETRY

Typeset using Centurion 10pt
by David Keay
83 Old Sax Lane, Chesham, Bucks HP5 2TE

and printed by
Antony Rowe of Chippenham, Wiltshire

INTRODUCTION

SURVIVORS' POETRY was founded in 1991 by four poets who have had first hand experience of the mental health system. Funding was received from the Arts Council of Great Britain to organise a series of poetry workshops and performances and to produce this anthology of poems.

Fortnightly workshops have been held at a venue provided by Mind in Camden and performances of poetry and music are organised monthly at the Hampden Community Centre near Euston. A number of external performances have taken place by invitation from various day centres, hospitals, MIND open days, art exhibitions and East London Polytechnic - we are still receiving requests for touring performances.

In March 1992 the Arts Council awarded SURVIVORS' POETRY a further grant to carry out an extensive national outreach project to promote further similar schemes in the regions of the U.K.

Poems have been submitted by workshop participants, performers and from various survivors from outside London.
54 poets and kindred spirits have submitted poems and illustrations for this anthology. Poems range over a wide field of subject matter and encompass many styles.

Survivors of the mental health system are a disadvantaged group within the community, frequently denied access and opportunity. In common with other disadvantaged groups survivors of the mental health system have a unique voice and experience to communicate to the world. Our poetry has a right to take its place alongside other forms of radical poetry.

The original inspiration for SURVIVORS' POETRY derives from Frank Bangay of CAPO (Campaign Against Psychiatric Oppression) who organised numerous poetry events and published poetry magazines with great love and dedication throughout the 1980's without receiving funding or official recognition. Frank Bangay is now a principal organiser for SURVIVORS' POETRY.

Recognition and thanks are due to the Arts Council of Great Britain for providing funding, in particular to the vision of Bushy Kelly without whom this project would not have been conceived.

This anthology presents the work of many poets and artists. We hope that it will inspire other survivors of the mental health system to organise poetry workshops and performances of their own throughout the U.K. to demonstrate the quality of poetry and to help dispel fear and prejudice.

SURVIVORS' POETRY
April 1992

One great challenge for survivors is the establishment of our own identities. We are not only survivors of a mental health system that regularly fails to meet our wants and needs. We are also survivors of social attitudes and practices that exclude us and discount our experience. Many of the identities society would have us assume - the mental patient, the vagabond, the tragic victim of disease - are ones we would never choose for ourselves.

Individually and collectively, survivors spend a good deal of time considering their lives. Being sorted out and collected up within the confines of a devalued grouping is an inevitable stimulus to this. Nonetheless, the questioning is genuine and vital. In what senses are we similar or different to other people, to other groupings? In what ways are we different to each other? For many of us, a central feature of our lives has been the way, at one time or another or even repeatedly, our perceptions, thoughts, ideas and feelings have been taken from us and possessed, processed, interpreted and described by others who have limited sympathy with who we are or who we might become. Does our difference lie in the quality of our inner worlds or in the fact that we got found out and were made to run the hoops?

One clear difference is our legal status. People who are diagnosed as having mental illness are always liable to be deemed incompetent. Because our problems and distress are seen as mental illness, we can be removed to another place. We can be kept there against our will, we can be given treatments that we have specifically asked not to have. Because we are different the law sanctions this. The implications of such incompetence and the socially appointed powerlessness that accompanies it are far-reaching and lie at the root of our dilemma. Although we are mad for a season we are marked in perpetuity. The standard response to our distress sets us up beyond society and sets us at odds within ourselves. The challenge we face is to repossess our experience and to reclaim our dignity and value as citizens.

Survivors are not incompetent. Nor are we devoid of insight. Many of the problems we share with other disadvantaged minorities - unemployment, poverty, isolation - are the result of discrimination rather than incapacity. But we need not deny our distress to achieve acceptance. The boundaries of approved experience are narrow enough already.

Through poetry and music, visual arts, writing and action we must fight for a broader understanding, a re-evaluation of individual experience.

Let the struggle continue.

Vive La Difference.

Peter Campbell

INDEX TO POETS

BILL LEWIS

THERAPY ROOM

Joe's making a stool
i'm weaving a basket
someone's making coffee
Dee says *I can sing*
and she does.
Jane won't make an
ashtray
Arthur's sulking because
the priest wouldn't re-
christen him *Jesus*.
Jane still won't make
an ashtray, instead
she becomes a dog
ggrrr Woof woof WOOF!
Dogs don't make ashtrays.
Dee's singing the
national anthem
Arthur blesses me.
Sydney hasn't spoken
all morning, or yesterday
or the day before,
gggrrrr Woof Woof!
Shit said Joe
I'm going to discharge
myself from this place
it's driving me mad.

realising what he had
said, he starts to laugh
i also start to laugh
the man on my left
(who didn't hear Joe)
starts to laugh as well.
we all laugh.
except Sid who wants
to die (and means it)
then we had coffee.

PRAYER

1

i do not kneel.
not, i hope, because
i am a proud man
but for the fear of
pride, and the
dark glamour of
outward signs.

besides humans are
always on their knees
before God.
especially, when
standing.

2

if i chant a poem,
and the audience
suddenly realise
it is they,
not i who wrote it
then i'm praying

when i take my
place on the
picket line and
someone gobs
into my face

and i look up
and see
not an enemy
but a different kind
of victim
then i'm praying ...

let my voice
be a cobblestone
smashing
against a
riot shield.

LIZZIE SPRING

FOR M.

There you are
a wreck of a man
though tender and true
your strength of the ox has deserted you
and, in your weakness, you feel ashamed,
shame that others should see you this way.

Remember the day I broke down,
the shock in your anger:
"Hey, but you're tough, lady,
tough guys don't cry."
I answered, "They may not,
but they probably need to."
Well, your body's breaking down now,
can't you see it's tired,
tired of being the tough guy,
can't you see you're tired.

The I Ching says, 'No shame. It furthers one.'
So, let the half vision be,
speak the half words,
walk blind.
The colours floating out of focus,
allow yourself, tender and true as you are,
the luxury of being a wreck of a man.
No shame. It furthers one.

THE PROPER LIFE

Be brave.
Courage, mon ami,
throw your mark,
stake your life on it.
It's not worth
rolling in the dust
when you could be

living
upright
and whole,
striding into the universe
with love on your back
and truth by your side.

SAM STEVENS

DESPAIR

When the world opens its mouth
I stand paralysed
on the edge of its teeth.
The great black hole
gapes its unwelcome
as the sun kamikazes
over the rim.
Man's last cry
Echoes through space
And the whole closes up
like a wound.

ROSEMARY DILLON

THE BEDROOM

My clothes are empty
Hanging as they do
   So still   So still
   Without flesh
   Without form

Outside the wardrobe
They suggest shape and form
   Imaginary events
   Taking place within them..

Dreams of confidence and happiness
Curve their design
   Cotton and wool
   And "manmade" fabrics

Carefully washed - from
Charity Shop and Jumble Sales
Size fourteen
Size twelve

While some are slung
Over a chair
Evidence of impatience and bad humour;

Soft black, flower prints, pale blue
   One dress slip
And burgundy for special occasions

My bourgeois weapon
That I cherish
   And then feel guilty about
    Looking at poverty in Finsbury Park Underground Tunnel
   Putting things in order
   And closing the wardrobe door
   I close my eyes

   And imagine Laura Ashley
   Even Dior..

      Dreams too expensive for ....

SEPTEMBER LIGHT

September light remains inert
in the early afternoon.
I have a dragon-fly for company.
What quality in me compares
to its powerful vulnerability, its innocence?

Silence a blank for my questions.
Chew over the old ideas.

Fresh blue-and-powder clouds
turn to tired pearl of an evening.
Summer didn't really happen,
and darkness gives me fear.

DAVID COOK

BEN

You were sleeping by my pillow when I left,
When I returned your were lying
by the door mat in the lounge.

I knew, instantly, it was over.

I cried spontaneously,
just like I'd seen Emily cry when she heard
about her mother's death.

You looked peaceful,
Your unseeing eyes no longer needed,
Your mouth ajar,
Fully stretched out on your side.

Eleven and a half years we lived together.

I stroked your face, I stroked your mouth,
I closed your eyes,
I stroked your tail.

I curled you up in a cardboard box,
Wrapped the box in plastic bags,
Put you in a black rubbish bag.

A spiritless body, clinically disposed of.

I cleared up your bowls
Washed up your place mat.

I felt sadness and relief.

I wish I could have spent more time with you
in the last two years,
I hope you'll understand.

I have your photograph
From sunny days long ago,
When we used to sit alone on the balcony.

You were with me each time
the child inside of me screamed,
And through the rock-bottom of April 1989
When Emily came to stay.

Ben, 1980 - 1991, Cat.
Aged 15.
Died 8th November 1991.
I love you.

LAURA MARGOLIS

SEEING IS BELIEVING

I saw Jesus in the Garden
High on Panadol
I was sweating and fevered
But I still saw him,
By a rusty wheelbarrow

I could not bear to look
But I remember
The sackcloth robe
The long brown hair
The ancient face.

Now, out of favour
With the Family,
Friends, even Foe,
I sit alone with Jimi Hendrix and
Cigarettes and coffee
Waiting for time to pass.

Is there life on Earth?
And is there Intelligence?
For I cannot see it
Therefore I cannot believe
But I did see Jesus
By the rusty wheelbarrow
And the Garden is still there.

STEVE BREWER

THE COLLAPSE

It didn't disturb me,
Cosiness and security in a room;
Playing records, drawing, reading,
Surrounded by confidence.

Hours could pass by...
Insularity haunts me,
Difficulty making friends.

I carried things too far:
Silence always seemed to be a virtue;
An accident unleashed a whirlwind
Strutting up and down the room.

The unbearable anxiety,
Loss, a loneliness
Difficult to compromise.
The room turned into
A Largactil dungeon,
Inescapable net of morbid contempt.

A disaster that nearly drowned me.
Meandering in a daze;
No grasp of time,
Trapped in an unbearable chaos.

The need of genuine help,
How many can obtain this?
Friendly, understanding people,
People you want to talk to.

The hospital can be very difficult:
Seeing the shrink
For five minutes a week,
The fly-by-night nurses -
The worst ones stay,
The pleasant ones leave.

Having known warmth,
I recognise cold
People with frozen doctors and nurses;
No wonder people are in crises!

A Tree of Life

I want to be a Flower
I want to be a flower

that blooms in the sumertime
that can survive the winter chill

The buds on trees half open in the spring warmth wondering if they are strong enough to come out and face the world.

but as time pases their strength grows encouraged by the warmth and sunlight they open up and Flower giving back to us little pieces of ourselves; peace of mind, peace of heart and spirit

FB
March 92

FRANK BANGAY

GLIMMERS OF LIGHT

Hiding in the shadows we feel safe
the mind flashes back to happier times
avoiding nightmarish memories
and a voice says
there are glimmers of light my friend
there are glimmers of light.

Blank walls block out signs of future happiness
still we look for signs
thoughts fumble over regrets
losses that leave emptiness
the longing to feel again
anger, sadness, anything.
I took my turn at trying to save the world
I took my turn at trying to protect the cosmos
I believed that I was made of rock
but really I'm made of china
or something like that,
something that will break so easily
into so many pieces
sometimes seeming too fragmented
to fit together again.
Where is the hope in this journey through darkness?
we keep on searching
we keep on searching.

Alone in a city too big for comfort
too many people
too much loneliness
the spirit gets lost under the noise and clatter,
you can become part of the crowd
and fade into insignificance
or you can express your craziness
and get singled out.
I seek spirituality,
I seek peace and harmony,
Where is true friendship,
Where is love?

Sometimes I want to escape from this competitive age
but there is no sanctuary
just a return to the psychiatric ward.
We pay a high price in our search for enlightenment,
sometimes we try to pay with our lives.
I hide from loneliness in a cold but crowded public bar,
I numb heartache with too much alcohol,
I stagger on in drunkenness,
unaware, uncaring for the consequences,
I ease sorrow with a feeling of bloated nothingness,
tomorrow I will curse the arrival of another hangover.

Kindred spirit we search alone
through a world of inequalities
we look for meaning
we look for healing
we reach out for the stars that twinkle in a magical sky.

Madness comes but we can recover
with love and understanding
I'm afraid to be alone in my searchings
we get pushed and pushed
and then we explode.

Hiding in the shadows we feel safe
the world outside seems full of hostile images;
a darkened mind tries to relate to a blue summer sky,
the soothing green of trees
before they fade into autumn,
there are glimmers of hope
a voice keeps saying
there are glimmers of hope
so keep on believing
one day your spirit will be strong again,
one day your spirit will start dancing,

       dancing

          dancing.

January 1992
Dedicated to a cruel memory.

THEY SAY, THEY SAY

They say beauty comes in glossy packages
but all I see is a frightened girl in war paint,
They say monsters have no feelings
but I saw a monster crying the other day
and I saw a man hit somebody
while smiling all over his face.

They say some have
and that some have not
but who has the right to judge
and who really deserves to take the blame?
And you tell me this land of ours is free:
Why then do you look at me in that way?

HILARY PORTER

DON'T TRUST

Don't trust the moon -
I know she looks so reassuring
floating in the void ...
but let me warn you
of the mask she wears:
She swears allegiance
as she smiles benignly,
then fails me as she wanes.

Don't trust the sun,
his smile is a deceiver:
I've basked,
I've let him kiss my skin
till he falls into the night -
leaving me tortured
with an aching head
and burning back.

Don't trust the planets,
they revolve oblivious
to all our earthly needs.
The sages read their patterns,
their promises and threats,
whilst we, the earthbound puppets
hear, and hope and fear ...
and then forget.

Don't trust the earth -
It seems so solid
as we tread its dust ...
until it opens up and swallows
all who dare to trust.

NO SENSE OF DIRECTION

Looking forward
from the safety of childhood
life seemed
uncomplicated;

I had a grand plan:
First I would grow up,
forge a career
(art, I thought)

then, when I was successful,
a little flat somewhere,
independence.

And later, of course,
marriage, children
the lot.

Life didn't, on reflection,
deal me such a bad hand -
No, I just played it badly !
No sense of direction, you see.

With the advent of children
life took a new direction
but something was missing
and whatever happened to art?

What happened to poetry,
To the future so hopefully charted?
Still there, I think,
but life gets in the way.

Sometimes, while driving
I get lost and find myself
somewhere unfamiliar,
far from my intended destination ...

... and yet, occasionally,
that strange place is more pleasant
than where I intended to be,
and I think - *perhaps*
I'm not lost after all.

THE BURIAL

I bury the ashes
of last year's love
in the barren earth
and with it,
while the ground remains open
I'll throw in last week's dream.
Together they fall
into the stony ground
laid to rest
at last.

No tombstone marks the spot
No flowers to wilt and die;
only the loose earth
which I kick back into place
over last year's love'
and last week's dream.

I leave the spot
without weeping,
with no thought
but to seal in my soul
and shut out the rest,
to become a robot
not programmed to feel pain,
with an on/off switch
where my heart used to be
and a micro-chip
on my shoulder.

I turn and look back
one last time.
Soon grass will grow
over the grave
leaving no trace
of last year's love
or last week's dream.

DAVID HARLEY

LOGICAL ERROR

Body and mind
have both left me behind:
    all my conversations take place
    a roomsbreadth away: facts and faces
        sliding off the porcelain,
        leaving me tracking condensation -
it takes all my resources
to follow the cursor:
        text and subtext
        defy my comprehension.

The machine hums and creaks
much as before,
    synapses firing late,
    but hitting the right barn door:
        an approximation to reality
        as good as most, I'd say,
and who's to notice a few bytes
chasing unicorns along
        the wrong pathway?

        (somewhere along the network
        my chest is still raw
        from the cruel kindness
        of the stomach pump:
        a vacuum still aches)

Headcrash; Logical Error; Division by Zero;
the walls crowd a little nearer,
whispering.

I-LEVEL

Well, you did it, all by yourself:
you selected a particularly fine piece of elm
and sawed, planed, moulded and mitred,
sanded and French-polished it
into an impeccable frame:
then you climbed into it.

It's no use at all
hanging there at eye-level,
whimpering
and waiting for me to smash the glass:
what makes you think this is an emergency?

What I will do for you
is leave the room
so that you can just
                    disappear.....

(Exit, singing)

                    "You always hurt
                    the one you love..."

NOMADS

Trekking the transient tarmac:
overrunning the striplit watering-holes:
our days are spent underground,
operating machines,
carried by machines,
feeding and fed by machines.

The city is choking on travellers
who have forgotten their destination,
as if every hypermarket was hyperstocked
with canned lotus-juice:

we have forsaken the tents of our forefathers
to rebuild the caves of our ancestors.

DAWN BURGESS

ONE SUMMER AFTERNOON
I didn't even
tell
God, the Way
Celie did
because I believed there was
no God if there was
He wouldn't have let it happen
to a two year old?
    three year old?
    four year old me?
    would He?
so I wrote poems and
stories/my own therapy
splitting
the bits and pieces of myself
I sent
Them
jettisoning
high
high
in the air
but they came back to haunt me
the way dead ones can do
came back to me
down the phone
one day at work
sounding like starwars
sounding like starwars
coming to get me
coming to get me
coming
inside
me
one afternoon
one summer's afternoon
at home

AFTER THE BINGE

"yeah Catherine died but she took 104
laxatives a day
if i take two more
what difference
will it make ?
what difference will it make ?"

You tell yourself your period is due   that is
why you need diuretics
tell yourself these pills are only for
today/tomorrow you'll start the new diet

but the more you lose the further the goal moves
away from you
and with all the distance of a god the image
becomes seductive
a model of alabaster   thin
draped in silk/white
but it is a savage god

And you begin to purge
purge
purge
that fragile frame
until you send the message home
you send the message rushing
gushing out
of you in hellish moments
you send the sparks of hopes and dreams shooting
in the air and your flesh your
flesh begins to
burn
until you are burning the electrolyte lines
in your brain

(what you wanted ?)

You are tripping on the train of a
golden haired
dream girl
so right   so white

and you swear to yourself/say to yourself
never
dear
god never

again   33

PAUL MATHEW

SCREAMING AT THE DOOR
(WORDS FOR THE CRUELLEST HOUR)

How tough is the steel
Of your heavy heart doors
How firm your mettle
How iron your resolve?

Scratch myself with a pin
Poetry on flesh
So the feeling sinks in
With the words
Prick my veins
Let them know
So blood soothes
My anger
Prick my veins
Let them flow
So the blood quells
My hunger

So stainless your steel
How long will it last
How stain-free your conscience -
All the crimes of your past

KIM

UNTITLED

How powerful the emotions
                    can be,
A bodily creation,
Of sadness and elation,
From the gentleness
            of a butterflies wings,
To the painfulness
                of a viper's sting
From the highest height,
To the darkest night,
From the hardest hit
            of a boxer's glove
To the warmth and tenderness
                of someone's love.
From the coldness
                    of the frost outside,
To the touch of
                a hand close beside,
A mixture of happiness and strife
A mixture adding up
                to life.

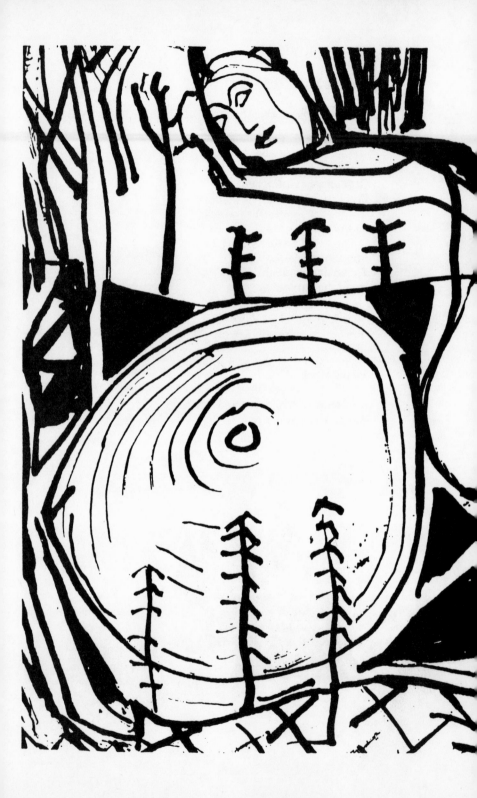

SARA RIVERS

TRANSFORMATIONS

I have been pushed along the banks
of narrow disaster;
clinging to the willow tree
and pear shaped laughter,
dressed in an eiderdown of
feathers
softly left to die
and lie,
in a solitary grave.

I have been pushed along the sea
of swirling ships;
dipped in the ocean of drift wood,
dressed in a greenish foaming bed,
held
softly
in the beams of
old rafters
and now
watch over you.

I have been drowned in the
hugs and kisses of old friends,
driven to the brinks of
new pastures,
dressed in a gown of moonlit sleep,
suspended
in the love
of the here
after.

I am being created, made anew,
to shape these words to you,
to allow love to flow
and be true.

RAZZ
LAUGHTER IN THE WORLD

Here's your fear and it's crying out loud
You're buried in your feelings
Like you're buried in the crowd
your eyes that notice everyone
especially the girls
is living for the moment
when there's laughter in the world

But a terror lurks inside you
Like there's bailiffs at the door
Your creative juice is frozen
Like a joke you've heard before
Only this time you're not laughing
Only this time it's revenge
Only this time you're in trouble
Only this time you're no friend

Come to me in silence
Come to me in tears
or come to do me violence
Through the voiceless rage of years
Years, I can't depend on
Days when shame and lust
Say there's no point in trying
Still, there's something says we must
'Though we're just bits of magic dying
Returning into dust
And still the fists are flying
And still there is no trust!......

O, and here comes your fear and its crying out loud
You're buried in your feelings
Like you're buried in the crowd
Your eyes that notice everyone
Especially the girls
Is living for the moment
When there's laughter in the World
I need some laughter in my World!

PEOPLE IN PAIN (DO PAINFUL THINGS)

In Wood Green shopping city on a Saturday night
Two teenagers got drunk and went to look for a fight
They could have found each other with their eyes shut tight
It should have ended differently but one had a knife
Jim staggered off bleeding he'd been stabbed six times
And Eric added Jim's name to the list of his crimes
He can hardly remember it, it's one of those things
But people in pain will do painful things
People in pain do painful things.

And Jody and her parents danced to different tunes
They never understood her, locked her in her room
They told her in the Devil's fire she'd be consumed
Between her guilt and need for them her anger bloomed
She headed for the city but she landed on the rocks
At sixteen she was living in a cardboard box
Now she's given up thinking what tomorrow might bring
But people in pain will do painful things
People in pain do painful things.

And everywhere you look you see a world of lies
And people getting laid off for the bosses' rise
You catch another headline and surprise, surprise
Crime is really popular, it's on the rise
There's always someone looking for someone to shoot
But the big fish get away with it by wearing suits
Yet they want it even tougher they want more control
They want to bring back hanging and suspend the dole
Well, they could bring back hanging,
they could pull those strings
But people in pain will still do painful things
People in pain do painful things

So, let's keep it strictly personal let's avoid the facts
Let's build a world on secrecy and see who cracks
Let's try to pack the chaos in a filofax
Let's tell you that you're paranoid and then attack
Forget about your childhood, forget about your past
Forget that it's legit' and then the die is cast
'Cos in a world that lacks humanity it's hard to be
And no-one's ever paid much for my poetry
But, I keep on doing it, that phone still rings
And people in pain will do painful things
People in pain do painful things.

RUMOURS IN THE AIR

Once, I stood in a dark place
Too dark for shadows

Where was I, where were you?
There were rumours in the air

It was a backlog of old invitations
Promises of light
Of the dark peeled back like a garment is
From skin
Promises of light
A room and a view
To put myself in ....

A kitchen appeared
A jumble of objects
And a steaming kettle
Flowers that need no words of mine

A sunset that beckoned
Outside the window
Voices that flared
Outside the window

While upstairs, that good friend
of mine
Is dressing to meet the World

I am part of this
A part of this World ....

But once I stood in a dark place
Too dark for shadows
Where was I? Where were you?
There were rumours in the air.

JOE BIDDER

VICTIMS & VAMPIRES

I told you about those victims:
poor bastards who can't help what they are,
tragic souls who can't do anything
needing money, support, food and love.
I told you about those victims.

They told me about their mothers
who didn't understand, the fathers
who beat and raped them as kids;
about orphanages which underfed them
and foster homes that didn't provide.
And they told me about their lack of's:
lack of love, lack of money, lack of understanding.
They told me what it was like being a victim.

Did I tell you about *those* victims?
The one's who creep into your life,
their lack of self-respect
means they have no respect for you.
Every hand-out accepted without a smile,
every positive stroke - a burning wound.
And when you've given all you have
they're angry, complain you don't understand,
that you enjoy your power,
that you victimize .. them ..
Did I tell you about those victims?

I didn't tell you about those vampires.
Evil bastards who latch on so tight,
whimpering while they drink,
then wipe their lips on your breast.
I didn't tell you how they keep on coming back,
how they always come back to make you feel guilty;
how they prey on your vanity,
how they cling to your shirt;
how their vulnerability makes you vulnerable.
I didn't tell you about those vampires.

Did I tell you about those vampires?
Attracted to your energies
when they have none themselves,
who always seem to be around,
who always seem to be around.

When victim becomes vampire ... you become victim ..
and what can you do but turn into a vampire yourself?

ILLICIT TEARS

Tears stream silently
from deep earth springs,
memories trapped
behind forgotten walls,
released in undefined sorrow.

Too long, concealed
the sadness that you are;
too long, disguised as
the rock you could not be.

Sand is less disturbed by quakes
than the mighty granite;
fluidly adapting to nature's force
unlike the rock which cracks.

Now tears flow copiously:
ducts undamaged by wasted years.
Yet odd, the flow of salt on cheek,
odd, the sense of misplaced shame.

Perhaps walls will collapse,
revealing long lost truths,
that struggled with the soul.
Perhaps the child will be released
from chains of time and person,
permitting tears to nourish
cracked earth and bring forth fruit.

ANNA NEETER

TO A FRIEND WHO COMFORTED ME IN TIME OF MENTAL CRISIS

In this bewildering wilderness I turn to you,
To the caress of your sweet words, your hand
That holds the stabling influence, the balm
That calms the salt-filled weal;
This burning inner anguish that I feel
And seek to understand.
Only the scarred, the sensitive possess
The kindred knowledge of the loneliness
In trying to pursue what I'm about;
Can still the doubt of whether it is worth it all
To heed the call I can't ignore -
Of people needing people more and more
In this impoverished world,
One of the conscious and degraded few
Who've walked this road of cynic-moulded pitfalls
Oft' before.
And so I turn to you...Forgive me, friend
If in my screaming mind I've over-stated things!
If I have set my sights on seagulls' wings
Only to bitter find there's oil upon the sea, -
I do not wish to drag you to the depths,
The insidious snare with me.
Keep flying friend, in sunlit air !
Give me the courage to return up there.
Thank you for all the joys, in such brief time
That you have shown; your gems
Cradled in the warmth you give,
Kindling my fire once more, - the want to live...
Knowing I'm not
Alone.

THE STUDENT OF PSYCHOLOGY

You were so gentle, friend, that I allowed
Removal of the strands of my defence;
That kind cocoon, which Nature spins to guard
Emotions lacerated by life's hard
Relentless thrusts that pierce us in our time,

The warmth that lit your laughter slowly stirred
The myriad colours dormant there within;
In loving hands that fragile web unwound
And from the shadows I emerged and found
A light and bright domain, unknown before.

Songs welled and spilled, zestful at times, some sad,
Such as I'd never sung with any man,
As we discovered new and vibrant chords
To play, like windswept trees or placid fiords -
A feeling world of sound and sense and touch.

In different lights and temperaments you moved
The facets of my nature in that strange
Kaleidoscope that holds the inner me,
Until I spread my wings, uncautiously,
Revealing all their patterns, without fear.

Then in an instant, taut, concise you pinned
Creation down with reason; joy with doubt;
Set on board to study and observe,
Anaesthetized in part, yet every nerve
Aware, seeing your form beyond the glass ...

Lesson: Reflect, recast

This too shall pass

FERENC ASZMANN

THINGS ARE GOING OK
(I'D HATE TO THINK GOD WAS HUMOURING ME)

When someone has died
it does not mean that they are dead
its just that you haven't seen them for a long time.

But this time gets longer
it shows no sign of ending
You don't meet the dead person in places
where you would
when they were alive
and you get older and older
and the memories change
and the dead person does not get older
they stay the same age
forever

as you try to remember:
they are not dead
it is just a state of mind in your head
Life goes on
So how can they be dead?

I expect to walk around the corner one day
and meet someone I know who is dead and I will say
"I thought you were dead ..!"
and they will laugh "ha ha no such luck"
and we will go into a cafe and talk about reality
and share cigarettes.

CONSENSUS

"Would you mind doing all the boring and dirty work
While we enjoy life to the full please?" they asked

"Not at all," they cheerfully replied
"It's all we're fit for anyway"

Strangely
No-one seems to remember this conversation.

MARTIN BROWNLEE

UNTITLED

Many among us speak for the insane,
But very few answer our questions
About life.
In our hearts we know we can win,
Shake off our oppressors
And live without fear.

In each other's arms we shared our bodies.
Gentle words gave me hope.
But in my dreams I return
To dark places in mad cities
Where we are all agitators and revolutionaries.
We battled with words, spontaneous anarchy.

- When I wake, the dreams are gone.
I lie beside my lover,
Together we flew from hostile worlds
And cruel prisons.

AT DENBIDGE HOUSE, SUMMER 1987

I am walking slowly back
From the edge of sanity.
A little man listens to all my excuses
No need to lie any more.

Coffee and roll-up reality
Spaces between visions
I took time out from Hell
To sit with a friend.

ON THE RUN FROM TOOTING BEC HOSPITAL

Passed another litter bin
Poor pickings from tourist treasures.
Soup kitchen blues, Red Cross blanket
Wrapped around me
I sleep in the park, just another dosser.

DEBBIE

UNTITLED

she took the stone
she squeezed.
out it flowed,
anger purple life.
stream,
i never knew it would
laugh,
it took me by surprise.

she lay upon the sand
she burned.
still it flowed,
amethyst pearl bayonet.
die,
i'd never seen the like.
smile,
the preachers turned and fled.

****

Hell descends upon eyes
Eyes that strain to see
Madness rules
Minds that want to be free.

Heaven smiles on the face
Faces that scorn
Pale upon the scorched earth
Another creature is born.

Reality falls fast on lids
Ripped by the messages of time
Blood appears
She glances through the rhyme.

PAULETTE NG

THE CHILD WITHIN

Tonight I touch a deeper part within
It is myself
Touching myself
My heart is open and I feel the pain
It is sweet, it is joy and anguish together
And the healer finds expression in my tears

So much sadness in the soul of the child
I open my arms to the pain
The pain is the child
And I welcome them both tonight
For this moment there is no anger
Only a profound acceptance

I hold the feeling - not too close
Daring not to clutch at this precious thing
I feel the beauty in the sorrow
And enfold the suffering child
Holding her tenderly within my being
She enters my heart
And I surround her with love.

THE OTHER SIDE OF VISION

Silent within silence
The strong cradles weakness
Hidden beyond perception
Behind well rehearsed smokescreens
Yet beneath the dispassionate mask
A volcanic force
Longs to spew forth its pain
Whilst behind unfathomable eyes
Battles rage amidst the burning lava
And some lonely spirit
Blinded by the ashes
Holds fast the secret
Of a sad and private grieving
So well guarded...isolated...
Eternally
On the other side of vision...

THE MENTAL HEALTH RACK

You've taken our minds and we want them back
You've put our humanity on your mental health rack
You've stolen our will, you've denied us our rights
You say that we're too sick to know
            that what you're doing's right...

But is it right to lock us up alone in an 8 by 6 foot cell
Is it right to drug us senseless, push us deeper into hell
Is it right to kill our feelings,
            is it right to numb our pain?
You say .. "yes, this is the way
            we will make you well again.."

We'll intimidate and analyze, we'll stop you in your tracks
We'll put you under treatment .. the psychiatry attack ..
Yes, we'll put you under treatment on our mental health rack
And we'll shape you into what we want, what society decrees
Then we'll teach you to successfully suppress
            all of your needs ...

But don't ask us for the answers, don't question our authority
We're the big white chiefs ... the gods on high
And you're just in the minority ...
And if you should prove difficult, not want to play our game,
We won't accept responsibility...
            it's your illness that's to blame

Yes, if you should prove difficult, start noticing the cracks
We'll increase the dose and turn the screws
On our mental health rack.

And in the end you'll have to see that we are always right
But if you don't agree with us we'll lock you out of sight
Yes, if you should discover our psychiatric lack
We'll lay you out for more dissection
On our mental health rack.

Then we'll just twist your minds a little,
put some blocks on your humanity
We'll just screw you up and wring you out,
saying this way back to sanity ...
Yes, we'll screw you up and spit you out,
saying this way back to sanity ...

So.. if you want to keep your freedom
Your integrity intact
Stay well away from those psychiatrists
And their mental health rack
Yes, stay well away from those psychiatrists
And their mental health rack ...

The Mental Health Rack 1992

DAVID KEAY

DELIVERED
moving slowly towards the door
he was the type who can
i wasn't any more than a parcel
in the palm of his hand...
and he did
...labelled in bold felt pen across the lid...
with approving nods
...second class...
from the psychiatric gods
...handle with contempt...
he offered his wares
...contents may settle in transit...
contract clinched
at the first attempt
...but who plans it & who cares..?

OUR ROOM

picture the scene, arm in arm
dancing in street, having a rave
with just a slight tremble of the feet
to avoid the bottles, tossed our way
from the safety of a bridge too far
invisible in the darkness of noon
"sing if you're glad to be gay"
should you wonder then, when
britannia waives the rules, only the mad fools
stray from the safety of the closet
in the corner of our room.

FOCUSING
as i opened my eyes
to a lifting mist
a woman in white
found shangri-la
halfway around my wrist
imaculately dressed tonight
darling
your fading face
you're fading fast
and one final lapse
we see spike collapse
your fasting face finally fades from focus
forever

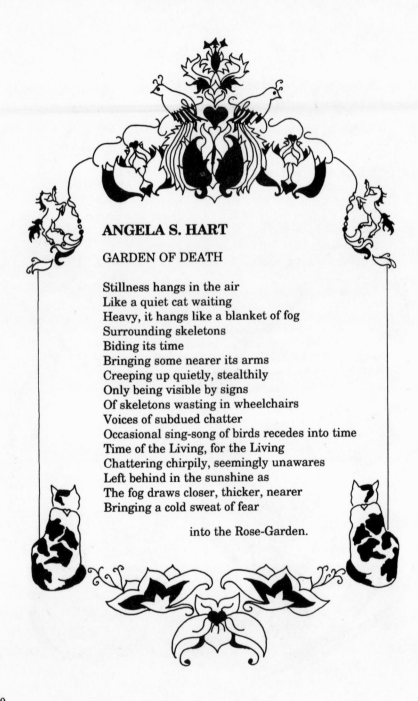

ANGELA S. HART

GARDEN OF DEATH

Stillness hangs in the air
Like a quiet cat waiting
Heavy, it hangs like a blanket of fog
Surrounding skeletons
Biding its time
Bringing some nearer its arms
Creeping up quietly, stealthily
Only being visible by signs
Of skeletons wasting in wheelchairs
Voices of subdued chatter
Occasional sing-song of birds recedes into time
Time of the Living, for the Living
Chattering chirpily, seemingly unawares
Left behind in the sunshine as
The fog draws closer, thicker, nearer
Bringing a cold sweat of fear

       into the Rose-Garden.

WOMAN TAUGHT ME TO HEAR VOICES

Woman taught me to hear voices
Taught me its all right,
Not to be afraid of the demon and the night
Chattering away, there still in my head
No more Largactil, I'm too easily led

Joan of Arc is talking, Woman want to be heard,
Can't shut us up with tablets, ECT, or White-Man's Word,
'cos Woman taught me to hear voices which want to be heard,
Taught me how to love them, now I'm free as a bird.

I fly in the wind and take your pain away,
'cos I've felt your suffering, know how you feel today
I love you all 'cos I also love me;
'Cos Julie taught me how to be free.

PETER CAMPBELL

DRUGTIME COWBOY

Nutters
Get
Compulsory sunsets.
Wall to wall landscaping of the soul.
Always a rugged coast,
Salt-flecked but liveable.
Always a hero looking west,
Going on about
The forward march of science.

You can have your sunsets
Cloudy bright.
Bright. Bright to cloudy.
Or extra bright.
With cloudy intervals at intervals
And something special for that tickle
Of psychosis.

You can have them
Any way you need.
But always orange.
Perpetual Orange.
And always.
Everlastingly.
Dull.

Nutters
Get
To stand at the window
Drinking the sunset down,
Tasting no rain.
Feeling the cracks in their spirit
Silt up.

Nutters get compulsory sunsets.
Always start writing back
Wish we weren't here.

IN YOUR WARM ARMS

In your warm arms
The day came in less like a vagrant
Selling tins.
Less like a loon
With a milky skin.
In your warm arms the day came in
Whispering.

At your neck
The day could seem
Less like a tinker's autumn schemes.
Less like a harvest standing green.
In your dark eyes
The world could seem
Welcoming.

The toss of a cold city.
Handsome strangers.
Encountering the gap between ideals
And the steamless beat of logic.
Arguing, winnowing
Waiting
For the sound of your feet.

In your warm arms
The night came in less like a hawker
Overspent.
Less like a gambler's discontent.
In your warm arms the night came in
Whispering.

MR. SOCIAL CONTROL

THE END OF HISTORY

Girders wrought of ingot steel,
A clanking derricks's final ring,
Bricks as red as dusty blood,
Foundries blasting molten ducts.

Lowloaders overturned and burned,
Shopfronts shot through, amok of guns,
Barricade soldiers scowling for skirt
See the city cinder in sicking flame.

Something's got to happen soon.
Industrial dream of grinding halt,
Dreamt of last evacuees,
Turning heads to join the flash.

Optic fibres flickering cryptic,
Pumping trance of acid hits,
Gaudy malls array with gifts,
Peppermint fondant sickly drips.

Clingfilm creased, the death of skin,
Motorways jammed and silent streets,
Housebound grasp of sky TV,
President hails new era's peace.

Dreamt of last evacuees,
Turning heads with pinefresh flash,
Dreamt of whimpers, dreamt of bangs,
Woke up overslept for work.

ARREST THE POLICE

You've been cut by corners,
And pushed by buttons far too long.
You've let the lightswitch switch you off
And the microwave turn you on.
You live life like it's rented,
But you don't need a new lease,
Cos it's yours so get your own back
And arrest the police.

Make war on war and bomb the bomb,
Judge the judges and trouse the trousers,
Publicise the public,
Lock them out of public houses.
Bathe the bath and toast the toaster,
As God prays to the Beast,
And tell the telly that you're off out
To arrest the police.

Don't believe in anything
If it doesn't believe in you,
Subject, object, dialect,
It's nonsense but it's true.
Prohibition is forbidden,
So steal back your beliefs,
Cop the shops and shop the cops,
Arrest the police.

Refute the future, pass the past,
Cos you're present in the present.
Companies arm the army,
And they govern government,
So turn the world the right way up,
And at the very least,
Fuck the fucking fuckers,
And arrest the police.

SINEAD

LIFE IN A COUNCIL ESTATE

Multi-storey
Council blocks
Tower over
The ant-like people
  In the street
    Far, far below...
This is what the multis saw
    From their lofty height...
    Balcony upon balcony
      Tier upon tier
        of tiny rooms
          cell-like in the
            vast city.
Long queues
  of huddled people
  wind-whipped
  waiting for a bus
    that never comes.
Lads, macho
Skinhead...
Heavy boots, white braces
Pink Punk hairstyles
Searching for identity
    in that featureless city.
"Paki - Get Out!"
Scrawled in greasy crayon
Beneath the broken window
of the frightened shopkeeper
Beside the Council Flats
    by the chippie
    in the city
Where the multis stare
    uncaring down.

LUCY LANT

THE GRAVE

I sense your figure standing above me
"Rest in peace" whispers through the pressures of your feet
But the earth is dry
And I wonder
Do you ever cry for me?

I cry up to you
"How can you ever substitute me?
Our passion was so real!
All others are diversions from what was really meant!
How we really felt
In the unguarded, unpretentious moments!"

How are you?
Suspended in your half-truth
Your distractions
Your back-tracked ways
Your preconditioned enthusiasms
Your repetitive beliefs
Your unchallenged, safe life ......

I have died to love you in its purest sense
At least there's a wholeness now
Not a half-way house, no emotional mess
At least my death is a simple thing
Clean, uncomplicated
True ....

Those roses and lilies remind me of the life that I lived
Bloody, thorny, cut-down
Here, the Passion Flower
Is abandoned
In the wilderness of your absence
Water me!

PAUL GERHARD

MESS

It's getting rather late,
I'm coming home to greet her,
ready rather neatly
to look her in the eyes
whilst telling her the usual little lies:
Will it be an office party
or was the train delayed?
did I bump into dear old Charlie
and have a jar or two?
I'm trying to forget
Chrissie's caught up cleavage.

Getting to the block,
up the same old lift
to the usual floor, into the apartment,
I call out her name,
and find there is no answer.
There's a light on in the bedroom,
Where I look in to find:
The one I really loved,
the one who loved me too,
the one I took for granted
in all my slanted little ways.
She's lying on the floor prostrated:
Overdosed and dead!

How does it feel to be
empty, angry and beat?
Is this the corpse I've created?
Is there a carcass on the street

yet?

SAFETY IN NUMBERS

Walking the streets with something to hide,
going to arrive at somewhere or other,
sooner or later, with people I know
not to share that something I hide.

Passing a pongy tramp - by himself on the street -
railing aloud to himself, and to anyone else
who cares to listen to ashes of argument
lost in the turmoil of alcohol anguish.

As people pass by they totally ignore
what flows from his lips to their ears,
and is lost to the fact that no-one's concerned.
Like baring your soul to all those around.

who show no response - not even to scoff
at the price you might pay to get to the state
where you're baring your soul to all those all around.
Needless to say,

nothing is said of the thing that I hide,
as I leave him behind in my stride and my mind,
I wonder if he's in a capable state:
Has he walked many miles marooned by his meths?

Does he realise himself what he's babbling about,
and to whom he is appealing? Maybe if no-one's the wiser:

Safety in numbers is found when that number is nought.

Sooner or later
with people I know
not to share that something I hide,
I will know how to make conversation.
As I dwell on the fact that I'm not the same sort,
walking the streets with so much to say,
and no one to listen. That slight of tension,
to think once, laid back split-second
clearly, before the words that I say
and the way that I say them
come from a knowledge inside:

Safety in numbers works well when that number is one.

PETER STREET

ASTRAL PROJECTION ...

Ghosting out of my body:
escaped from B Ward.

I velcro on my harness,
click and screw tight the karabiner
and thread and sew the nine-mil' rope

through a silver figure - eight:
leaning backwards onto thirty feet
I spark down the building wall.

Outside the nearest chippy
I eat fish and chips
out of yesterday's goal mouth
while Ian Rush dandruffs salt
from his shoulders.

For the lads;
new legs and spinal chords
wrapped in a tray.

1964

Never be late, was knocked into me.

Fifteen minutes I sat there
waiting for the Careers Officer
where posters of young farmers
with calves scarved around their necks
walked towards me

in between the Royal Navy piping me on deck
and the sickly smile from the boy
stood over his lathe.

I ticked Footballer, Postman, Forester.
The man with the mustard tie vomiting down his shirt,
brylcreemed hair (a greasy tarmac road
with a white line axed down the middle)
landed me with labourer in a slaughter house
saying "epileptics with literacy problems
don't get work, you're lucky !"

Epileptic ! the farmer wanted his cow back
the Navy pissed off
and the engineer put two fingers up !

BUSHY KELLY

FROM DARK TO LIGHT
(or a case of mistaken identity)

Cut with a knife the blood oozed forth
ever so gently, slowly at first.
A few droplets squeezed out to lie
complete on the work surface
in the kitchen.
Domestic harmony.
On the plate lay two halves
perfect in their succulent pattern
waiting on a table.
Symmetry of red,
red into brown,
brown into darkness.
Darkness of night.
The lamp was lit, glowing warm yellow.
A message on a beermat, words.
The first scrawlings of a child's name.
A wooden bowl and a bunch of flowers
lay too on that table bursting forth,
plants spreading their leafy splendour.
Quiet bliss.
Peeping into the wooden bowl
lay another mystery.
An Autumn apple, a dead leaf,
disturbing the relative harmony
of this domestic scene.
The fruit had been cut,
lying on the table unshared.
A shut door.
Flowers, pure in their whiteness,
pinks only faintly glowing through
the stillness of the night.
A bottle of whisky was drunk
to send the thoughts racing swiftly.
It was a case of mistaken identity.
domestic harmony broken.

Domestic harmony - a lie.
Darkness of night - the truth,
where dreams could roam free away from prying eyes.
Quiet bliss - a sense of space,
the excitement at the development of a child,
another person.
A shut door - pain at the way
this path to self-knowledge,
of shared trust is closed so firmly.
Domestic harmony broken - the lies sat
so firmly on the table between the participants.
Shared knowledge that could not be accepted,
let alone communicated between them.
In silence the distance remained.
Coldness - a family split.
Not daring to admit it was so.
Normality - the pretence that relations
continued as usual.
The decision was made.
No victory for anyone,
who cared to look at it clearly.
Suddenly right and wrong
were not the main issues anymore.
In sympathy and tears
words could be spoken
that meant something at last.
Maybe.
The sub-text revealed for all to see
that dared to question a reality posed,
on the surface only.
Domestic harmony.
Darkness of night.
Quiet bliss.
A shut door.
Domestic harmony broken.
From dark to light or a case of mistaken identity.

THE LION

Truncated heads.
Amorphous masses.
Dislocated limbs.
History.
The history of what?
A lion with its nose cut off.
Smashed.
To spite itself - to spite others?
Hush.
The dreams are gone,
The nightmares close in.
Hear the roar of the lion.
Exploited.
Condensed into a life
that knows no pride except that of memory,
memory which cannot be quashed
by a superiority,
expressed through violence.
Listen to the silence.
Stung - with a lancer like poison.
Sometimes a quick death,
more often slow,
the poison seeping through
with a razor like edge.
No way to dull the pain
except through a laugh
and a belief that the spirit
cannot be crushed,
however many bones are broken.
Remember the silence
At the end of a roar.

IAN KELLY

FAMILY MOSAIC

You can't describe the effects
Of a bomb
Till the bomb has landed
And settled
In fragments
Of a hole
Like a chipped wall
   Shattered
But complete

You can't describe the effects
of a family
Till the family has landed
And settled
In fragments
Of a whole
Like a chipped mosaic
   Beautiful
And complete

JAN J.

TO RELATE OR NOT TO RELATE

Deep
Too Deep
Misunderstood
Unloved
Loved Too Much, 'Cos I'm Too Deep.

Too Deep, Too Honest
No Time For Me 'Cos I'm Too Deep
Too Honest.

Heavy - Not Light Enough
Hurt, Alone With My Hurt
Hurts Being Alone.

Lots of layers like layers of clothes in winter.
No one person wants to look at them *with me*.
One layer is only one part of me.
But no one person is willing to see all parts of me
and for it to be reciprocated.

I feel exposed - undressed
While you all look fully clothed.

Want to - Don't Want To.
Scared and Not Scared.

MICHAEL FRANCIS

A DAY AND A LIGHT YEAR

Visions of lights that blink in black
Visions of stars that shift and sink
As I sift the sand my blind eyes dazzled
With mind ablaze my brown eyes think.

Gods have created a silver sun
In her beauty she has shone
But not a disc she smiles tonight
But light enough for lovers' leap
Yet not death, but a hilly climb
My eyes stilled on lovers' peak
Then wish and think on mountain stars
A day and light year seen afar.

THE MIRROR, THE MASTERESS

The merry-go-round ceases and there is joy
As ease and peace from within starts
A goodbye kiss blown to fires of hell
Hands warmed on the flames of a heart.
No wish to drink from wishing well
While walking across morning dew
Hand-in-hand combat on common ground
Treading the mud is now beautiful.

The first note of spring, singing from outstretched arms
Evening rain, each drop strengthens the root.

To the lake
suddenly still
Top 'o hill
The silver one shines
She is you
She is truth
She is love
She is the mirror. The Masteress.

PREMILLA TRIVEDI

UNTITLED

Sleepless nights, enveloping despair - guilt,
Guilt at being me - black, female, poor,
part of a large family
Part of an even larger society,
resounding with racism and rejection.

Valium, psychiatrists, falling more into the abyss
of white man's medicine.
Hospital, enforced activity, constant cajoling
To fit their categorization of me,
All the time denying me *my* pain - *my* hurt - *my* confusion,
Reinforcing my "badness" at feeling these things.
Isolating me, alone, with "my" problems.

Unexpressed anger, increasing guilt,
the silence growing louder.
Largactil, locked doors, ECT, eventually stillness.
Sinking deeper and deeper into the sanctuary of insanity:
Beautiful - silent - still - feelingless - internal death;
Pushing back the screaming agony
before I infect them with my poison -
The poison of my blackness, my culture, my very being;
All wrong, all contradicting the norms of their society,
all disrupting their ordered world.

And in the end I saw it their way, the guilt was mine.
So I tried - and battled - and pulled myself out of it -
And buried myself deeper, keeping me inside,
Smiling nicely, acting right, colluding with them,
Ensuring *their* equilibrium was maintained, so I have
the privilege of existing in their world -
of experiencing their values, their beliefs,
Their prejudice, their power.
What does it matter that I died in the process?

What *does* it matter, one more black neurotic female,
One more drain on society, what does it matter?
To them, nothing -
And ultimately to me it must mean nothing too,
Otherwise even existence becomes impossible
And internal death can only be mirrored in external reality.

LEAH THORN

MESHUGGEH *

Maybe meshuggeh was the first word I ever heard.

I certainly heard it more than any other word
as I was growing up.

I was meshuggeh. Everything I did was meshuggeh. Anything
that in any way deviated from a strictly defined norm was
meshuggeh. Problem was, the norm changed regularly. Enough to
drive anyone "crazy".

Everytime I described my reality in a way that displeased or upset
anyone else, then that was meshuggeh. My reality was constantly
being challenged, threatened, denied.

"I'm not happy"   Meshuggeh!
"I'm scared"   Meshugges!
"Something awful's happening - help me!"   Ach, meshuggeneh!

Meshuggeh is when you have your nose pierced and your parents
cry and wail, "We'll never be able to face the neighbours again"
and "Why do you always have to hurt us?"

Meshuggeh is a man exposing himself to you and your mother
hitting you round the face for being schmutzig

Meshuggeh is not being able to put the rubbish out unless you've
got your make-up on

Meshuggeh is being groped at a party and when you make a fuss
being told "You're too nervous"

Meshuggeh is believing it's your fault you got raped.

Meshuggeh is nearly dying and being told off by your parents for
causing them aggravation

Before long, I took on the label meshuggeh and began to believe
there was something wrong with me.

84 * Meshuggeh is Yiddish for "crazy", "mad".

FINGER PICKIN' GOOD

Look at my hand
It'll tell you

The story's there
                    in the serrated cuticles
                    the uneven swirls of skin
                    down the side of the thumb
                    the pink soreness
                    a badge of my pain
                    red shield of despair

I peck at a finger nail,
its irregular pointiness irritating me
Smooth it off. Make it perfect.
Perfect it

Have to keep these fingers under control.

Pull insistently at the skin that just won't come
but thrusts up to taunt me

Nibbling. Fiddling. Prising. Picking

My fingers are numb
until the skin tears
"Now look what you've done!"

My hand goes in my mouth
to stifle a scream
silent
like Munch

My teeth grind with the effort of chewing off
the ever present flaps of skin.
Red, yellow, pink thumb
comforting as I run my tongue over the roughness.
Polished skin, broken and re-broken over many years.

I can't not, you see.
I love the pain as I flick my fingers across the flakiness.

ERIC PENROSE

WHAT'S IN A NAME

Part 1

What is in a name you ask
What is in a name?

Remember all the names there are,
Remember all the names.

For all the names that come to mind
Remember all the names.

These names can come from far afield
These names can come from far.

For many names there are, there are
For many names there are.

Part 2

You heard it said
You have it known

How many names there are !

But now I tell you what they are
I tell you what they are.

Each name hides a thing;
This is something each name hides.
From within the name
Is what it's not.

So this is the name
And this is the game.

DINAH LIVINGSTONE

NERVE

Roof leaks, stop it with sticky tar,
thick and black like a babe's first shit.
Wall cracks, and we imperfectly plaster it
with a slapped mixture of pinkish powder.
Light bulbs break, we are in the dark,
drains block and the sludge reeks of decay.
Propping and prodding keep the frail pad cosy
and fickly hold the primal soup in check.

Neither can we ban weakness from the bonehouse;
I bleed, I ache, I alter every day.
Skull lurks, disintegration stalks us,
I am unwomaned when I've had no tea.
I only find my centre now and then,
when good animal spirits give a shove
or where beyond tiredness joy slips in:
ocean, eros, here-earthly union, love.

And when I spin in centrifugal panic,
feel dizzy as the velvet night wears thin,
I do not flee the hound of heaven frantic
but from the hole I fear is where my centre should have been.
String snaps, I collapse, am disassembled.
How now scrap antiquated parts; add; see
whether this heap of heterogeneous junk all jumbled
fits back together another way?

Constantly. This is the price of every poem
and of living, every time it snarls up, wisdom.
The permanent point is cordial
being both membership and individual.
It needs a great heart not to deviate into religion,
courage to utter, endure chaos, utter anew,
nerve not to give up making and, with knots between,
thread the blood-red garnets, despite what death will do.

ROWAN TREE

Three boulders of granite
step over the stream
where the steep path hairpins
at the head of the combe.

Islanded here, splendid
in all its full-berried vermilion,
filtering sun through eager green,
glowed the rowan tree,
magic and exigent
as when for True Thomas
it marked the choice of ways.

I kept still, filled my eyes,
listened to water
and for red deer,
waited to be told. What?

When the bright ordeal burnt out
I munched cold bun and cheese.
Later in London another rowan
shone among drab donkey brown
of terraces and pavement slabs
recently rinsed by rain.
Clearer with second sight.

SONG

Mistakes heartache
unexpected defeat
burnt all black
dead beat.

Fire charred the heath
death dried the heart
They who hated this earth
have deeply scarred.

Yet deeper the seed
love sheds its life.
Blood stopped stone dead.
Moist warmth unfurls leaf.

My hope is red petal
heart beat.

NEIL SPARKES

THE FEAR THAT LIVES INSIDE

dead drunk living on the floor
    get up and ask for more

you've been drinking
    but you don't make a living

in the wilderness
    outside most peoples' reckoning

looking for a way back in
hitting the bottle and losing your mind

living from day to day with no way out
    the prisoner of 4 walls

    get outside

    the sun is pouring down

in our foolish rooms we build love
    or smash our lives with lies

in foolish rooms we'll die
    caught in a moment of gladness

do you then begin to say thankyou
    to the ones you love the most

do you then begin to find the words
    for all the things you feel about your life

    see the madness
    feel the fear
    that lives inside.

PHONES AND DOGS

standing
        on the street
in the night
        waiting to use
the telephone box

a man walks up
        to wait
                with his dog

"how old is your dog?"
        i ask the man
his eyes roll inward
        wary, defensive
the dog all muscle
and balls and brute snout

"you shouldn't ask
a man the age of
his dog, it's like
asking how much
money he earns"
        turns and walks

the dog looking back with
eyes like heinrich himmler
on heat

ugly little bastard.

LICK YOUR WOUNDS

dawns early rising
gave me blisters
mouth sores, ulcers
skin razored in a flash
of suds
            towelled, the
bathroom is at odds
with the rest of the house
tiled stillness for the
morning's retreat
coffee for the mug
sparrows perched
on the sill
egg and bacon
grill for the rashers
kitchen full of frying.
throughout the day
i return to the
cold bathroom
gloat on the chipped enamel,
plugs, taps, lick my wounds,
sink in the tub
unable to face the days.

COLIN HAMBROOK

DREAMING THE ABSURD

And I wonder if I'll ever be sane
dressed from head to toe
In a madman's frame.
And I wonder if I'll ever be whole
For to be myself
Is to be a fool.

I am dancing,
I am a spinning tree,
Whispering an ancient melody:
But there is a bureaucrat
In the toilet of my mind.
He's counting the faeces
I've left behind.

And I wonder just who I am;
swimming through the air
on a leg and on an arm;
and I wonder how it can be
that humans put a price on this life.

I am flying,
I am a cunning man;
Questioning this meaningless sham
But there's an autocrat
in the attic of my mind.
He says that I'm important
but I don't know just what he means.

And I wonder just what's going on,
for my atoms are dust
and I am a memory
laughing, I am a weird bird,
soft and dark,
dreaming the absurd.

SEX, DEATH AND POETRY

Make sense, Make sense
Says the doctor in my head;
I've built me this bed
And I can't seem to lie on it,
Die on it, pray on it,
Who'll heal this emptiness:
My dad in his domain?
Making jokes at my expense;
He says I'm a silly joke
To be dispensed with, dealt with
Bored unto death wishing
For a reason and a purpose.
A stench of sickness in my gut
And little fishes in my balls,
Stirring up a storm in my loins,
In my brain, I can't escape this pain
Of illusion, confusion,
My mum on her mountain
God in her head, calling up a dread
of living and giving
it was all too much like sinning
But they never talk about
What He does with His penis.
Tears in my mouth
and semen in my hand
I'm rigid with grief
Just wanted some relief
From judgement and deceit
But it feels too much like running
and running and where is the fun
in my day on this path
So who who knows how this little boy
Will find integrity
and say in that last breath
That his life was a poem.

ROSALIND CAPLIN

RAIN -

it did not stop all day

shrouding the world in greyness,

clutching with slippery fingers and never letting go..

A subtle, heavy mist descending in crystal droplets,

    on and on..

Glossy pavements mirror a sunless sky

while rows of coloured umbrellas stream like a turbulent ocean

along a waterlit street

   like lilies floating on a tidal wave

to disappear, like extinguished candles

into the Silent Clouds.

JAMES TURNER

THE PEDESTRIAN

I walk to work. The route: the same, always;
  Past houses (terraced), gardens (small, with cats),
And people (regulars, occasionals).
The distance: one mile. Two sisters - or pals -
  One short, one tall; with Downs syndrome, and hats:
Hand in hand they stand at the curb and gaze
Expressionless, waiting to cross: most days.
  A thin black kitten: weeks have passed since it
Last came, cautious, tail up, to sniff my fingers.
A naked woman (still the memory lingers):
  I saw her, on the phone, just once, sunlit
Through frosted glass, her pale limbs ablaze.
  Perhaps she gave just the effect she sought -
  Or was the glass less frosted than she thought?

WHO STOLE YOUR MIND?

Who stole your mind when you were still a child?
    Who built a fence around it, locked the gate,
Mislaid the key, then looked at you and smiled
A loving smile? And why? Thus domiciled
    And tamed, your thoughts - confused - would soon stagnate
And sicken pale as covered grass. So mild,
Obedient, you became. Your charm beguiled
    Us, hid your sadness, fear, and (later) hate.
Now feeling (bruised) and thought (deliberate)
Cohabit in your soul, unreconciled.
Past cruelty - denied, forgotten - seems
    To have vanished; but trodden snakes revive
To snake unrecognised into your dreams
    And waking life, your destiny to drive.

JAN MARSHALL

UNTITLED

There is a great Aloneness within
an emptiness now
of dead creatures and poisoned soil.
Blackened air and polluted seas.
The animals, our friends are alien to us
NOW

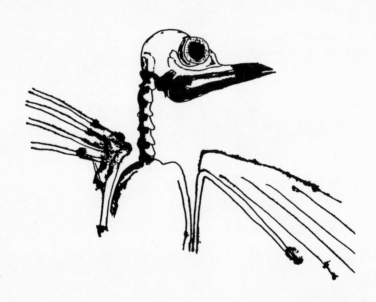

PSYCHOLOGICAL DISINTEGRATION:

Insanity, Neurosis, Epilepsy and Psychosis
archaic terminologies that don't seem fair
They talk in secret languages like they don't even care
These people, the doctors; retainers in Hell
their ritual requirement, to the sound of a bell.
The clients inside all afraid like strangers
they crowd then let go to a solitude danger
Each, a hostility of surrounding worlds
taken in hand like little boys and girls

JOHN RETY

THE KITCHEN CHAIR

Think of the kitchen chair,
Then having thought,
Write down what you have thought.
Then having written down what you have thought
Think about the kitchen chair again.
Then having thought about it
Long enough
Ask yourself this question:
Has the kitchen chair changed
In your mind
Since you have written about it?
Read what you have written,
Then sit back and think
and having thought,
Write it all down.
This will keep you ungainfully occupied
for the rest of your working life.
They will point you out at Compendium:
"There goes the man who writes the kitchen chair poems.
Everybody thinks he is the new Maya Kovsky;
If you want my privatised opinion
I am sick and tired of his kitchen chairs -
Kitchen chairs this, kitchen chairs that,
are there no other chairs in the world?
Chairs of this and Chairs of that, Boardroom chairs,
Chairs of Grants and non Grants,
Chairs bolted down at the DSS - He'll soon find out
and anyway if he wants to make a living out of writing
There is more money in bedroom chairs".
Having heard all that, think again, write it all down.
Await no payment, no thanks, no fob watch of olden times.
Clear off and get out of the kitchen.

JUDY KESSLER

SAME BUT DIFFERENT

There may be more than the here and now
But I'm here and it is now.
With wheels that take my silent feet
Don't you go for a ride at times?
I fight to be understood.
Sometimes you are lost for words
I am a disabled mother
Some mothers lead disabled lives
I urinate, bleed, laugh.
I cry and live life.
I fear you sometimes
Do you fear me?
I am here
Working for acceptance

SPRINGS ON MY WHEELCHAIR

Spring is coming
And the flowered, recycled air
Will once more seduce my rumoured self
Into the curdling day.
My wheely feet's silence will take
The grey eating road into a forgetfulness
Of the Winter's shiver.
Too long now my eyes have focussed on
The square box of glass humanity
So I will explore the explosion
Of the ordinary day.
I will see tender birth in gardens
And tender new birth in plastic prams
See laughter on a pansy flash
And book-end cats reclaim their territory.
There will be week-end markets
Then tea and fresh scones at
The cottage on the quay
And once more, I in my chair
Will gallop up Kent's fragrant Spring face.

GEORGE PARFITT

HUBRIS

The gods repay hubris. Always.

For a small poem of depression calmed
a price. Not immediately
(the gods do not lack humour)
but when a sense of immunity
has come and lightly skinned
the impetigo of despair.

Then the gods stir and smirk,
confer briefly and send,
with irony, intense replay,
but teasingly. A morning doubt
grows, then for hours gouts
of heavy grey. With this
the gods repay my hubris.

REMISSION

I should make ceremonies of these things
to survive;
should stroke the black dog's hair
until it lies ...

Teasing the strands of a Cabernet,
refining grains in the coffee filter:
such may save
or other relished smallness.

Firm set of new shelves, red brickdust
whirled free by the drill's bit;
stone-edging a long-arid flower-bed
content only with the best line I can -
this may help lay flat the fur,
dull the spears at the temple-bone.

Quiet walkings even, repeated,
drawing smiles and greetings; sightings
of new shapes in trees, in clouds and buildings
may, truly attended and received, ease
the jerk of nerves and vocal chords.

An eye to the anarchy of hedges,
dust at picture-rails, on books,
tile-smearings - all of this,
made ceremony, may help me miss
the shoals of suicide,
but must be loved for themselves:
salvation in small satisfaction.

PAULINE BRADLEY

JANE   a song

chorus:
Jane, Jane why did you have to go away
Jane, Jane I miss you so
Jane, Jane I wish you could have stayed because
Jane, Jane I loved you so

You were far too clever for this world
You never told a lie
Even when the truth was hard to hear
You'd often make us cry

And maybe it's selfish for me to say
I still want you here
I know you tried so hard to get away
You always made that clear

chorus:

Underneath that hard exterior
You were still a child
Who needed warmth and care and nurturing
And to go a little wild

And I know your life was a painful one
They didn't understand
Your folks they wouldn't give you space to be you
They always would demand and demand   but

chorus:

This was your final suicide
The one that did succeed
But if you only knew how much we cared
You might not have felt the need

Well perhaps you're better off where you are
For no way out could you see
You're not confined in that body you hated so much
Now that you are free, you are free

But Jane, Jane - I know why you chose to get away
But Jane, Jane - It's sad to see you go
Jane, Jane - I think of you each time this song I play
Coz Jane, Jane - I still love you so...
.....Jane

JASON KINGDON

JOURNEY PART 1

I wonder how I came here?
What steered me on my way?
Did I have a choice on this journey?
No, I had no say.

How did I grow into this body?
Who's jeans do I wear?
What is this history before me?
Oh questions, questions.

These questions I thought I'd answered,
My life has no meaning,
How deluded can I be?
Not man enough to face,
The world would go on without me.

When I look around for answers,
More questions I now find,
The sure thing now I know,
Many people are unkind.

There seems always to be war,
A famine or a flood,
No wonder prophets prospered.

The news is hardly new,
Somewhere someone's baby's crying,
All the poets rhyme with dying,
Strange how it does seem to fit,
I wonder why the words
Were made to sing so sadly,
Gladly,
Is not the ending for the next line that I write,
Maybe, I'll leave it open ended,
Hanging in the air,
Suspended in the breeze,
Tipping off my tongue,
Dancing out the door,
On the last train out of town,
Yes,
Maybe I will leave it open ended,
You will think of something to rhyme with sadly, I'm sure.

JOURNEY PART 2

I once left my house,
Intending not to return,
I'd run out of food,
Run out of money,
Run out of clean clothes,
Run out of gas, electricity,
Run out of hot water,   although I find myself in it.
Run out of patience,
Run out of luck,
Run out of sense,

I'd run out of my house,
Intending not to return.

At the time I was confused,
I would ascend into the stars,
Maybe, this is how death takes you.
When you run out of control,
When you run out of hope,
Out of faith, anything to believe in,
When the only answer is leaving.

If you don't know what for,
There's nothing behind,
So why not leave for more,

I can cross the border,
Make it to the other side,
It will be cold along the journey,
I'll have to be prepared,
To run, to crawl, to hide.
Cross this gaping hole,
Stand a chance, I may survive,
From this life I am leading,
To the other great divide.

LORD BYRO

NOTHING

I know all about nothing
because nothing is my scene
I've nothing to my left or right
and nothing in between.

Nothing *is* something
but probably not a lot
unless of course nothing
is all that you've got.

I collect lots of nothing
bit by tiny bit.
But the problem is
I've nowhere to keep it.

I'm positively negative
nothing gets me down,
which is rather sad
as nothing's all around.

As this ode is all about nothing
then I really must insist
that the poem and the writer
probably don't exist.

JAN GUICE

PIECES OF ADULTS NOT LOST TO CHILDHOOD

Who goes there
in the dark of childhood?

Who held their hands
across eyes and mouths of truth?

Who took the sad little faces,
their own reflections,
then threw them away?

Wordless, sightless
they grope on
to find those things familiar
and familiar they feel
when found
put back together
their sore broken pieces

hot coals, driftwoods
pieces of people
slowly recognised

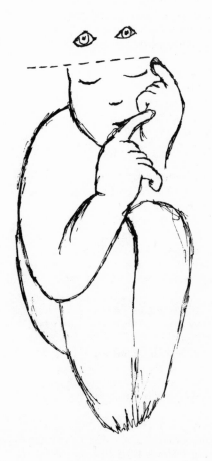

FRANCESCA BLASS

GRIEF IS A BIRD

Grief is a bird that sits
Oh, so heavily on my shoulder
Stony eyes viewing my world
Focus vacillating points of view
Stream through and before me.

You will never leave me,
But lift off -
Hover just a little -
Propel me not in magnetic force
Eyes to the world
Nailed to harness - a Mother's loss.

Gone, sweet young blade, sapling,
And I still asking why and how
I inhabit this world.
Fathomless garden of trees
Dancing an eternal rite
In the restless winds of change,
Whispering singly and together
As with all things in their otherness.

Lift off, hover just a little
That I too may move the flesh and bone
For Spirit -
Slave over the question
Why he came like an alien to this land
In gentleness, perception, anger,
And left before his time.

Move off my shoulder -
Hover just a little.
Let me dream I have no chains,
That this is yet my twinkling time.
I too must have my seasons, moods:
Invisible made concrete in the garden.

LAND OF PROMISE

Bittersweet the scent of blossom in the land

Land of Promise where my child was born

> Sorrowed ocean of the skies
> Furrow deep in sharp ferment
> In vying human argument

> Yield Mother Nature's way
> To strokes Old Father Time may pay?

> Or Stand

> Expose

> Unnatural sacrifice
> > Youth's romantic caste aside

> > The burning of a Star ...

Bittersweet the scent of blossom in the land

> Healer - old magician merely mocks
> As day is born
> Our living turn of dark to light
> Swept feint ripple on the shore
> Whisper on the wings of tide

Bittersweet the scent of blossom in the land

> Daleks we -
> Of mortal casement, human brain
> Tossed by this infernal time
> Eternal essence dare divine
> Rise phoenix from the flame

Bittersweet the promise of blossom in the land

ERIC IRWIN

MINSTREL SEA

I hear the sea
Playing her tired lament
With muffled drums
And feel that she,
singing her changeless chant
On hidden tombs,
Now sings for me.

Her minstrelsy
Mourning the sombre mood
In cadences
That capture me,
Swelling her salty flood
With soulfulness
And sympathy.

Deep melody
Melting away the wreath
Of murkish haze
Benighting me,
Bringing again the breath
Of summer skies
As sings the sea.

DREAMS

Sleep's lazy river slowly twines among
The Stygian glades where sometimes soft light seeps
To shine around the dreamer drawn along
Upon his drowsy raft on slumber's deeps;
Projecting varied pictures to his view:
One sheer delight, another dark distress.
And painted panoramas seeming true
Come subtly to the drifting consciousness.
Ethereal scenes - and scenes more real than life -
Heavenward hoist the soul or hurl to hell,
Portraying answered love or anguished strife
Till sad or gladsome, waking breaks the spell.
  Ah, my lost love, how sweetly sleep redeems
  My waking loss, when you're re-won in dreams!

OFFSPRING OF THE SNOW

Again the snow,
Stealthily falling
In the frigid night,
disguising ugliness
And pristine days recalling.
This same show
In morning's glare of white:
Trees in bridal dress,
Hushed footsteps come and go,
And eyes of innocence exclaim "delight".

Found on Eric's person:

...please remember this - as a consolation
A certain amount of loneliness is
essential in a balanced life. No...
Perhaps I should have written
"solitude".

It is only in the silence that you
can hear what your own heart is saying
to you. and if the silence is unbearable,
you are in a bad way. The man or woman
who must always have company is only
half a man or half a woman.

For we must face this tremendous fact -
THE FINER THE TEMPERAMENT, THE RARER THE SOUL,
THE MORE LONELY THE LIFE.

INDEX TO ILLUSTRATIONS

ACKNOWLEDGEMENTS

SURVIVORS' PRESS thanks each of the contributors for texts or illustrations published in this anthology for the first time.

For permission to publish text which is copyright material, we gratefully acknowledge the following -

Mixed Emotions (PROMPT Publications 1982) for *They Say, They Say* by Frank Bangay.

Hot Poetry No 5 (1984) for *Things Are Going O.K.* by Ferenc Aszmann.

What They Teach in Song (CAPO Publications 1986) for *The Collapse* by Steve Brewer; *Minstrel Sea* by Eric Irwin; & *Consensus* by Ferenc Aszmann *(Ghandi Versus The Daleks)*

Summer At Tooting Bec (Struggling Books 1987) for Family Mosaic by Ian Kelly.

First Things (Diamond Press 1987) for *For M.* and *The Proper Life* by Lizzie Spring.

Rage Without Anger (Lazerwolf/Hangman Books 1988) for *Therapy Room* and *Prayer* by Bill Lewis.

Rhythm of Struggle / Song of Hope (CAPO Publications 1990) for *Dreams* by Eric Irwin.

Matter of Life and Death (Zzero Books 1990) for *Illicit Tears* by Joe Bidder.

Mindwaves (Issue 13/14, 1991-92, published by MIND) for *Transformations* by Sara Rivers.

My Psychologist Sacked Me (Clerical Department, Maudsley Hospital 1992) for *Mess* and *Safety in Numbers* by Paul Gerhard.

Pieces Of Writing (Jan J 1992) for *To Relate Or Not To Relate* by Jan J.

Earth Poems (Jan Marshall 1992) for *Untitled Poem* by Jan Marshall.